MW00902411

TIME LINES: poetry and prose

Gloria MacKay

Gloria MacKay

Original title
TIME LINES: poetry and prose

Cover image
Based on Félix Vallotton's "Naked Woman Kneeling in front of a Red Couch"
and Clayton Boyer's "Genesis" wood clock design

Cover design
Sonja Smolec

Layout
Yossi Faybish
Sonja Smolec

Published by
Aquillrelle

Printed in the United States of America.

ISBN 978-1-329-59550-7

"Time really is one big continuous cloth, no? We habitually cut out pieces of time to fit us, so we tend to fool ourselves into thinking that time is our size, but it really goes on and on."

~*Haruki Murakami, A Wild Sheep Chase*

Table of Contents

TIME LINES: poetry and prose

Inadvertently

a candle dents darkness
the way a thumb
pokes bread rising
or the sun nudges
into a fog

wordlessly—
alphabets all over the world
floating in soup

timelessly—
clock tickings shunned
and fallen away

mindlessly—
over-kneaded clay spinning
reluctant to stop

silently—
how long is a moment
how soft is a day?

Gloria MacKay

Waiting for Time

The pause before a tock
is long enough to save a life
or end it. The future of a second
is as hard to guess
as the significance of a single tear
a bead before it dangles on a string
a note without a symphony
a star without a galaxy
a gasp, at last.

Left Hanging

The drive from my house, down the road
that winds around the highest hill
in town, is nondescript

faded ramblers, bland patches of land
a mini-mall with gaping vacancies
a few new homes clustered

but no grass, no barks, no bushes, no bikes,
no one to wave with, all by myself
taking pot luck with the jazz station

or simply driving hard and thinking fast
I feel a hill of people descending
and they all want my spot in the fast lane

on a long saunter home I face
patches of sky washed in celadon blue
and lean into watermelon clouds

dripping invisible mist — almost home
one afternoon, just past the last bend,
I drove eyeball to eyeball

with a vanilla yogurt afternoon
moon, the same one we each see
occasionally but obviously

not in a blue moon state of mind.
She looked a little pensive, though
so alone and so far to go

Gloria MacKay

Expectations

Should is a word of meditation
rarely graffitied
not often texted
seldom cross-stitched
bumper stuck

traded, tattooed
or chanted by lonely older women
unless prefaced by I
and kept in an apron pocket
like a Slinky ready to spring

I, for instance, should
make lists and not lose them
write poetry that rhymes
cook from scratch
stay married, find time

I should play bridge
it's good for my mind
but not three times a week
and knit gaudy little street fair sweaters
that make babies cry

I should finish every book I begin
including mysteries and Michener
and every spring, fill the same seven clay
pots with never ending red geraniums
and then bake a fresh strawberry pie

I should deplore violence, applaud
executions, speak the language
of cooperation and consent
Could you? Yes
Would you? Yes

Sign here Yes Go there Yes
Pick her up Drop him off
yes and yes and yes and yes
and, yes, I really should
bake a fresh strawberry pie

Gloria MacKay

Sipping Warm Milk

She flicks open her napkin and slips me a glance
What will you miss when you die, my dear?
What kind of a question is this
just before lunch
I say please pass the cream
Sugar, my dear?
You know I don't use sugar

Night quiet, sheets smooth, bed cool
I'm on the edge sipping warm milk
I won't miss anything when I die
that's what I should have said
instead of please pass the cream
I don't use cream

What's to miss?
I will be impervious, oblivious
a chalkboard wiped clean
One less slice in the toaster
No more rolls of the dice

What's to miss?
Stars? When it rained those thirty days
and twenty-nine nights in a row
I forgot about stars. On the thirtieth
night there one was
Twinkle Twinkle

What's to miss?
Springing ahead and falling back
The breath between a tick and a tock
a ding and a dong, the ring and the talk?

What's to miss?
How my sons will look when they get old
and their babies when they get old

and their babies' babies
laughing and dying in three quarter time —

For Pete's sake, she used the wrong word
It's a who not a what
Who will I miss when I die?
How long a list can I make
or should I say take?

Will I miss people I have not yet met
those who haven't been born?
What about the dead ones
I miss them now; will I miss them, then?
Will I miss myself?

How's that for tautology, dearie?
Next time I'll be stirring my coffee
and simply sidle it in. Who will you miss
when you die? She'll pat my arm
in that way of hers and sigh

what a stupid question
It doesn't make any sense
Please pass the cream I'll reply

Gloria MacKay

Dreamers, Beware

Real time tosses out moments
like a handful of bees … or corn
popping with the lid slightly askew

Between the aim and the fire
the I and the do
the pitch and the hit and the woo
planes crash, hearts start, bombs drop
legs cross.

An unexpected moment
is as hard to grasp
as a single tear without a cheek
a bead without a string
a q without a u

Sleep fitfully, dreamer
like a new mother sprint set for gold
oblivious to the ticks and tocks
under her feet …
real time flies.

I Should

Every morning, as I hunch over the counter smelling the coffee drip, 'should' springs out of my conscience as surely as my knee jerks when I tap it.

Immediately, I remember I should be making tea instead. I know they say it's better for me, but who is they, anyway? What good would it do. I don't know, but I should.

Should is the word that keeps me peeling potatoes when I want to go for a walk and then send out for pizza, the same word that insists I finish every book I read including mysteries and Michener.

I should make lists and not lose them, turn leftovers into soup, and memorize the language of cooperation and consent. Could you? Yes. Would you? Yes. Should you? Yes. Pick them up. Drop then off. Yes and Yes and Yes and Yes.

I should love my neighbor, keeping in mind birds of a feather should flock together. I should deplore violence and applaud executions. And every spring I should fill those seven clay pots stacked in the garage with seven red geraniums, same variety, lined symmetrically where the neighbors can see.

I should refrain from unsettling my family with unseemly behavior: saying bad words, not cooking from scratch, divorcing, wasting time. As a matron these days, I should look the part, but how should I define the role? Whatever I am in the morning, do I have to be it all day long? I suppose.

Gloria MacKay

Watching Poetry

I was …
this is what I am reading
at the top of poetry pages these days
I was …

or a similar coupling
linking someone's personal pronoun
such as I
to the past tense
sense of to be —
or even not to be

that much-loved infinitive
still musing through time
but not yet trendy enough
to sit at the top of the page
centered under the title
I was …

or butt up against the left margin
right below the title
so the reader perceives
the cliché
the way poets are doing it today
I was …

When I sit with a batch of words
I need an immediate alert
that we are going someplace.
How do I? love thee, ah
Do not? … go gentle
The moving? … finger
I wandered? … lonely
I care
you are
I am
we were
I was …

10

Off the Wall

I am a good deal taller than the little girl who once was me — a sepia child on the living room wall with bowl-shaped hair and blunt cut bangs wearing her favorite dress of soft-washed blue, cherries down the front and no buttons.

But at least an inch shorter than The Mother I Once Was lifting laughing babies high, knocking down cobwebs, topping a tree with a star, all on her tip toes and yet another inch shorter than The Matron I Became — ensconced in that new rambler on the beach, still standing pretty tall against a southern wind, hanging laundry high but feeling low.

I shrank perhaps another half an inch when I came to be the Divorced Old Lady in the gravely little condo on the hill where I was asked to dog sit for free. Why me? *Now that you're alone you could use the company.*

We wake up taller than we were the day before just for a while — then we shrink until we die. But we are the same people. I feel like I did as the sepia child, but where has everyone gone? Are they not the same person, too?

Gloria MacKay

Lost in a Mirror

I'm fine with a circus.
Down the hill from my house
a circus pitched its tents
every summer. Too dangerous
I was told, for a little girl
to walk there by herself,
but I could open my bedroom
window, smell the smells
and watch. When the big tent
went up the elephants helped.

We drove down there once
my dad and I. He parked and
bought popcorn. We followed the
sawdust paths and passed little tents
I never saw from my window.

The house of mirrors was where
I cried. Grown men strutting,
chests out, shaking their fists,
showing off. I could see myself
far away, cowering in a corner,
small and creepy-green. I forgot
my dad was outside waiting for me.

And so it is as time continues
I drift through gray spaces lit with
cautionary hints of yellow, on a path
without a map and no corners.
There is popcorn sometimes.

Slow Talk

Slow was a virtue parents used to teach their children. My dad was always telling me to slow down: I moved around the house too fast; I ate too fast; worst of all, I talked too fast.

In the evening he would sink into his overstuffed chair, pick up the newspaper, fold it, deliberately, so the front page was on top, and settle in without a rustle for a long, slow read. I would take this as my time to talk and since I had a lot to say, I talked fast.

"Slow down, child," he would sigh, looking over his glasses, chin on his chest. When my words kept bursting like popcorn he would slowly remove his glasses and slowly but more energetically repeat, "For God's sake, child, slow down."

In those days, slow was slower than it is today. No one could, or ever would, so it was said, run a mile in less than four minutes. Cars moved slowly enough even a child could read Burma Shave signs on the side of the road, and on a hot day when I opened my grandmother's cooler to finger the ice, the drips were a long time coming.

Slowing down is something we don't emphasize today. Parents keep two vehicles humming: to and from school (the bus is too slow); to and from lessons of one thing or another; to and from practice, for one sport or another. Families don't have time to be slow.

My dad did not push slow food the way he did slow talking, probably because we did not know what fast food was. The only eating out we did was an occasional Sunday stop at the Triple XXX in south Seattle. You didn't have to get out of your car, but it wasn't really fast food.

My dad rolled down his window, a pert waitress on roller skates took our order and skated it back on a tray which hooked over the open window. Sometimes it took a long time to get served, but the food was never defined by its speed. It was a Sunday afternoon treat, fast or slow.

Slow food, as regarded by some, means anything that takes so long to eat it is calorically self-limiting. Take nuts. While the average snacker devours twenty cashews a minute, we down only eight pistachio nuts because of the time it takes to break open the shells.

Pistachio is a slow food – along with celery, artichokes, barbecued ribs, steamed clams … and pomegranates, too. After an experience eating a meatball sub sandwich while driving on the freeway during rush hour, I would certainly add that to my list. Slow … but dangerous, as well.

I once read (slowly, of course, my dad did not approve of speed reading) that talking fast is also a health hazard, often associated with the Type A personality — that dreaded powder keg of tension and stress.

A group of heart patients were asked to read the United States Constitution out loud twice, once quickly and once slowly. When they read quickly their blood pressures climbed and their hearts beat faster than when they slowed their reading down. The final word is not in, but it looks like my dad was right to make me slow down, although his concern was not for my health. He wanted to hear what I said and read the paper at the same time.

Speaking of chewing, a new gum is supposed to improve our memories and help us concentrate. To be effective, we should start out with two pieces for a half an hour three times a day. Along with an ample assortment of slow food this could keep the health conscious chewing from morning to night.

I doubt if my dad would have tried it. It is rather expensive, and I know he would not have shared it with me. He didn't like me to have gum even if it was free. I chewed too fast. Besides, he would have said that forgetting is just very slow thinking — which just might be the next health fad, along with slow food and slow talk. I can hear him now, mumbling, "For God's sakes child, slow down. You're thinking too fast."

Backseat Cosmology

I would wrap myself in my dad's old maps
he kept in the glove compartment
in case he got lost
which did not happen often;
he seldom went far, and
when he did it was always to Minnesota
where my mother's family lived.
She knew the way.

I wanted to find my way too
stretching my arms wide over my head
like a scarecrow, trying to refold
dad's crackling map of America
in and out like a fan, then
set it on the seat and follow along.
Without a word he grabbed it
and put it away.

In all the years I went to school
I was never taught nor was it implied
that the universe, too, is unfolding
I learned this from a Woody Allen movie.
The boy worries "Someday it will break apart"
The mother hollers "You're here in Brooklyn
Brooklyn is not expanding!"
My mother felt the same way.
I'm not so sure.

Gloria MacKay

Elbow Room

Isn't it really the space between the notes
that makes the music and the room
between the letters which turns
the alphabet into words?

Surely our front teeth decree
their space, between, as rest stops
just for whistling
and hands can share
their finger space
for rings and string — and look

at books! Around the edges of the pages
is space where numbers coalesce
in solemn contemplation
like unexpected guests

and while we barefoot on the beach
upending rocks and holes and logs
where to stash the scattered sand
without the space between our toes?

why does the rumination of scientific men
— the ifs and thens they cogitate —
imply there is no space if there is no stuff
as though they owned it?

islands brushing, wrinkles mingling,
matter succumbing to mind
I have a memory of a face
don't touch
It keeps my universe in place

Shhhhh!

When you're home alone do you ever laugh?
I don't mean a quick snort at an e-mail joke
or a phone a friend tête-à-tête gone risqué,
and, by the way, an inadvertent cackle
with the canned laughter on a sitcom rerun
kind of afternoon
doesn't count.

What I'm asking is, when you are by yourself
in your bare-boned, unplugged,
air-cooled, drapes drawn,
silent as stone,
dog-free, no bird, childless home,
do you ever think of something so funny
you laugh out loud?

When there is no one to share with
wouldn't the congruent response
be to think about laughing?
I do it out loud …
Is this normal?
No one will know unless somebody tells.
Shhhh!

Gloria MacKay

Red Hats Are Coming

Be sad for crones with heavy fingers
with twinkly diamonds on wrinkly skin
and crimson badges of battle
perched on blue-moussed coiffures
slightly askew, like their smiles.

Stand back from women with outlined lips,
(shades carefully matching their hats) with no
intention to stay in the lines, like captive daffodils
standing limp in jars of green water.

Stay clear of clubbers clicking their pumps
like metronomes running amok
matronly legs in sausage-like casings
sashaying to a saintly beat.
Blatantly busy, busy, busy, little bees.

Shopping Mall Is a Four Letter Word

In winter I sprint to the entrance
bundled in woolens and down
and run into a face full of preheated air
Ah, warm at last
Too warm, actually
I unzip my coat. Take it off. Drop it.
Stuff it into a shopping sack
Sack bursts
I put on my coat
I roast. I go home

In summer I plod to the entrance
attired in T-shirt and shorts
sandals slapping against sweaty heels
and run into a face full of frosty cold air
Ah, cool at last
Too cool, actually
I buy a latté, tall, skinny, single and hot
I want my sweater
It's in the car
I go back.
I go home

Early is eerie
The information booth unknowing
the candy store dark
A woman pushes a broom
I smile. She doesn't.
A man clutches a briefcase
I nod. He looks at his shoes
I look at mine.
This is ridiculous
I go home

Later is weird
Revved-up women with clicking heels

Gloria MacKay

wailing babies
bolting toddlers
teens roaming in packs
Men limp on benches like fish
or as tense as wild cats
in strange basements

I want to go home but I can't find my car
Next to a spindly tree I recall
three lanes to the left of the bench
on the north side of No Parking
I end up in a different store
or go out a different door
There are no trees.
There is no phone
There is no store.
I want to go home

Hand Me Downs

that's what hopes are
something to leave the children
bereft of anything else
there's always that

hope floating in a faded corner
of a well-used pocket
displacing the give-away penny
let the good times roll

wishbone breaking days
taut as knuckles ready to crack
hope over our heads like a moon
or the moon of a moon

weary mothers at nap time
slipping away without a whisper
dry hopes, non-recyclable hopes
crackling like used cellophane

Gloria MacKay

After Reading Einstein

Where does truth go when it isn't being told?
Where is your lap when you stand
or your fist, when you open your hand?

Why do they say each snow flake is one of a kind
when some dissolve in the air
while others hit flat on the grass with a splat?
How do they know?
Answer me that

By the way
who are they, anyway
those who know?
I get it
Not who they are but it is me
Forget the form follows function
less is more cliché
That's passé
The new stuff?

Time is warped and space is curved
even without my elbow in a pomegranate martini
and my head quarking
like a roly-poly clown
on the floor to make babies laugh

All my thoughts are in there somewhere
Where else would they go
Explode out my nose?
But I can't say the words
Maybe they are in German?
I don't speak German
but I get it.

Uncuffed

I wash my black pants together
not singular, one pair, two legs
(a misdirected plural, for sure)
I have seven
fourteen legs
not identical, but almost,
spinning together
nine
if you count the slippery ones
black acetate and polyester
(I have two)
plus of course
the seasonal fleece
they fill the washer
fading into each other
like black holes
on dark days
in a crowded galaxy

then tumble dry
like unfolding children
and recoup
on wire hangers
double hung
above my shoes
lined up in pairs
heading for the ark ...
but only in their dreams

Gloria MacKay

Words ...

String around my existence
like twinkle lights
on barren cherry trees
usurping the peace of the season.

Hammering untested thoughts
on bottom lines of golden
rules and platitudes before
I am ready to speak.

Controlling my unkempt mind
like rubber bands bound
around faded business cards
whose time never will come.

Words are mere puppeteers
pulling my strings while I play
let's pretend I have something
important to say.

Three Little Words

As much as I love to write I stopped when my first son was born and did not try again until the fourth one helped empty the nest. It wasn't their fault. It was mine.

I talked too much, once I became a mom, butted in too often, stuck my fingers in everyone's pie and scrutinized every plum. My kids didn't have a chance to grow like weeds, I measured them every inch of the way.

Why did I make so much work out of mothering? Because I was management, that's why. I was in charge and if I lost control I'd be usurped by little people twice as small but twice as smart as I. Then what would I do?

I had never been a boss before: sure, I had stepped aside when they bustled by; I mulled over their memos; I observed their pale blue eyes looking through me, grazing the room. If I ever got to be a boss I figured I could walk the walk and talk the talk even before I learned to think the think.

Then, the first chance I got to be in charge, I blew it. I tried out for a position far beyond my experience. I knew I wanted to be a mother but I didn't know that I didn't know how. Furthermore, my underlings did not bring manuals. They preferred running naked through the house empty handed, as mindful as shiny bubbles.

Motherhood was ending up to be more than an eight to five job with no mention of weekends off or vacation. I told myself I was never going to write another word. Still, mixed into my thoughts like dust in the corners was the belief there must be a way.

This must have been why I spoke to them in short, simple sentences like a drill sergeant shaping recruits. Brush your teeth. Wash your hands. Eat your lunch. Zip your coat. Go to sleep. On a good day I punctuated with pleases and thank you. On a bad day, I'm afraid I forgot.

What I was trying to do, without knowing it, was to single space my mothering using very small type so there would be room at the bottom of the page just for me. You would have thought, with all the words tumbling through my brain I would have stumbled earlier upon the two most significant phrases a mother must learn to survive.

25

Gloria MacKay

The first? *I don't know.*

The second? *I don't care.*

When my four young sons clamored for dessert why did I snarkily remind them to clean their plates first (they knew I knew they knew that already) when I could have responded I don't know?

"Do I have to take a nap today?" I don't care.

"What's for dinner?" I can't remember (a mom must be flexible).

I could have done that. Backed out of the scene. Enjoyed the play or written one of my own.

These days when I am weary of gossip, bored with politics, overwhelmed with religion or simply don't want to talk anymore I practice these magical words on my friends. They have become my mantra, of sorts. Not that I was looking for one nor am I sure what the plural of mantra is, but now I have two: two sets of three little words that every boss mom needs to remember.

Currently, when I am asked to be a boss I do it by simply showing up. I mutter an occasional, "I don't know" or scribble a note declaring, "I don't care" just to show I am on task but I don't judge so much. I don't care so much. I make very little of what goes on my business.

And when I am lucky enough to be in charge of children I don't mess around with their pie. I'll sit on the floor a bit, smile a lot, speak every now and then, and listen carefully … even when they're not talking to me.

Hopscotch

Life is the only real game
but don't tell the children
Let them play unashamed
in their chalk drawn squares

hopping over flat rocks
button clusters, anything
that can grab a spot without
skidding over the lines

no need to reveal the
play-within-a-play cliché
no reason yet to read Hamlet —
wait until the rains wash away

their game, the driveway dries,
the chalk is lost in a pocket
and the markers become
as forgotten as castaway dreams

Winter Reflection

To die is to spend a night alone
with a power failure
in a wind storm.

The mirror above the fireplace
(my treasure from grandma)
splatters across the carpet

like shards of dead stars
how many times to flick the switch
but the lights don't come on?

how much squinting at the stove clock
to see but not see blackened time?

how much time passing does it take
before death tiptoes away
with blood on its feet?

Pick Your Pronoun

I know you're out there, all you they's.
What's the matter with you, anyway?
Your hair is too short or too long
Your pants? Too loose
or too tight and your skirts?

Up to your crotch or down on the ground
You don't fit in.
you've got to go
You're too far out, too fast, too slow

How do I know?
The we's told me so
I like their style, I'm humming their tune
I'm learning their lyrics ... not a moment too soon

They's pack peanut butter, we's do lunch
They's rent movies, we's see plays
They's go to regular school.
We's don't
but they used to,

when Education was well-groomed
grammatical, good-natured, genteel.
No rabble-rousers then, no fanatical fringe
giving our conscience a twinge
No passionate, out-of-control
questioning, skeptical, scholars
when a chicken in every text book
pecked the order:
white, yellow, black
Protestants Catholics, Jews
high, middle, low
man, woman ... period

Gloria MacKay

That was the way. Those were the days
Go ahead, snicker, all you they's
I've got God on my side.
How do I know?
The we's told me so.

Passing Through

and so we go –
two grains of sand
afloat in a sandal,
or flakes in a shaker
sliding slightly askew.

just a couple floaters
skittering over a watery eye,
or a pair of names stacked
in a hat holding hands.

thank you for the use of your hat
thank who for the use of your hat?
and so we go: shadow sisters
on the run, stretching and shrinking
which way is the sun?

Gloria MacKay

Threads of Memories

The wiggly touch of a baby tooth
dangling, hangs on my memory
like a pendulum, ticking
yesterday's time.

I placate the clock
reprogram the sun
howl at the moon
It's too soon

to unravel my past
scrape my brain like a pumpkin
splintering body from mind
with the unretracted claws of time.

come here my little chickadee
cajoled my uncle and aunt
when they were very drunk
schmile and show us your hole

and I was very young
standing open-mouthed
the scent of their wine trickled down
along with the bitter taste of their time.

my baby tooth swaying – going
long time passing – going
as I hum along – gone

The Chase

I can snatch a shred of melody out of the air
as fast as a bird snaps up a bug.
Words drift by like afterthoughts but that's okay,
I never expect to ingest the whole song.

A ribbon of sound spewing out of a truck
in the fast lane last Tuesday was an exception.
I caught the gist as easily as a bridal bouquet
but, unlike the flowers, this time I wanted a finish.

"You inspire me" purred the songstress
drifting past like a Cheshire cat sans the smile.
I pursued her, pedal to the metal, like a child at play,
intent on lifting the lyrics right out of my day.

You'd think I would come up with a line or a rhyme,
a who or a what, or at least a feel for the beat
but all I could hear was a roar as the truck sped away
leaving me laughing in the slow lane last Tuesday.

Gloria MacKay

And Then There Were Four

I collect words … a worthwhile hobby for a woman like me, one with neither room nor inclination for stuff (brooches, antiques, silver spoons and the like) and a reluctance to hang my passions on the wall.

My computer greets me with a new word each day. Occasionally I throw one in the trash as I would a cracked cup or musty paperback, but most words pile on my hard drive like fallen leaves. When I fear they will clog my machine I shoot them off to a cloud.

I tend to mark chapters in my life with pithy little thoughts, turning them over in my mind so often they become, I must admit, trite. This is what I collect, a set of my own personal clichés: reminders that I did the best I could with what I knew at the time.

My collection is smaller than most. For years there were three. The first has a Biblical tone, perhaps, or a Shakespearean ring. I can almost hear the phrase in the mutterings of Hamlet, except these are the words of a woman.

What is hard to endure is sweet to recall.

When I first came upon this I scoffed but it remained in my head as patiently as a book waiting to be read. As I was growing up there were times when I could scarcely endure my family: the year I cooked my first turkey and my dad insisted he stick his camera batteries in the oven just to "charge them up a bit"; the Christmas he had that same frayed accordion pleated camera turned backwards and took a flash of his nose and my mother laughed so hard she fell over, flattened the tree, and the baby started chewing on the tinsel.

As years passed a second keeper doubled my collection.

The best revenge is a good life.

This advice so heartened me I shared it with my children in the guise of motherly wisdom. "What is a good life, anyway?' snorted one son, in the throes of adolescent pain.

"You'll know it when you see it," I replied. The moment I said it I knew I sounded smug, but what is a mother to say when she wants to help but she can't?

And when it comes to revenge how can there be a good, better and best? What was I thinking?

Years passed before I dared pontificate a third personal cliché. The French say *c'est la vie*, Sinatra sings *that's life*. To my list I added

Loving your bargain doesn't make it painless to pay the bill.

I found these words, like a prize in a box of Cracker Jack, in *Sabbatical* a novel by John Barth. No hint of angry little ego or mawkish retrospection here. A statement of fact, tucked in my brain like a roll of tightly wrapped coins.

I intended these three bits of wisdom to see me through to the end. But there is one good thing about being a collector of words — there is always room for more (even if one resorts to parentheses).

I came upon a fresh string of words as inadvertently as discovering a four-leafed clover in the grass. It is almost too bumper sticker cute, except there is a Woody Allen "I am not afraid of death. I just don't want to be there when it happens" piquancy about it.

Wherever you go, there you are.

This is what goes around in my head these days. Just thinking it makes me smile, but I love to say it out loud, especially when I don't know what to say. Folks usually respond with a meaningful nod or a quick but gentle shrug of understanding.

Gloria MacKay

My Truth on the Loose

She bounces off walls and lands
on her feet like a cat,
slides through tall grasses
with the grace of a snake
and stumbles down stairs like a drunk

My truth on the loose
is as hard to control
as a kite and as risky
to grab as a spark

In the dark
on the fourth of July
mute like a mime
private as an afterthought

Pesky as a mosquito
on a muggy afternoon
no matter how hard I swat her
she will not stay away

She churns inside me
a dancer who two-steps alone,
a yo-yo singing, an arrow spinning
and where she goes nobody knows
most certainly, not me

How Far Apart Are an Angel's Eyes?

Cuttings from bed sheets curl around coat hanger skeletons. White pipe cleaner circles hover over skewered Styrofoam heads. Wings starched and sprayed within an inch of their ethereal lives, jut upwards, as inviolable as protrusions on a 747.

A woman, thin-lipped and wide-eyed with chin embedded on up-turned palm kneels before her creation. "Help," she groans. "I can't do this." She unbends and waves an arm flecked with aerosol gold. "Help." she wails. "I can't figure this out. Will someone please tell me — how far apart are an angel's eyes?"

Seventeen glue guns cool and seventeen women listen. One whispers, "I was wondering about that myself."

I don't know what actually happened next and the person who told me didn't know. I've always wondered how the instructor responded and how long those thirty six plastic eyes waiting around in a sandwich bag rolled their working parts toward the heavens. Was there a group discussion? Did the Baptists and the Unitarians agree? Do the Catholics think metric? Is there a correlation between angel height and eye spread? How tall is an angel, anyway?

If I ever need to know how far apart an angel's eyes are I will ask a child. Children know these things. A four year old might question, "Where do we go when we die?" Or "Who made God?" Or "Where do babies come from?" Kids don't know everything. But the children that I have met know that an angel's eyes can be just as far apart as the angel-maker wants to put them.

As soon as toddlers curl their fingers around jumbo crayons and their urge to gnaw on the art supplies gives way to the urge to create, they become artists.

They draw what they know: themselves, mommy, daddy and the dog. They draw what they don't know, a wedge of sun beaming from the top left hand corner of the paper, and to top it off they put in rainbows.

A child does not ask how long is a dog, how big is the sun, how many colors in a rainbow?" All children are artists and artists know these things. And they draw what they feel. An angry child can cut and paste the blackness of the universe onto an 8 1/2 by 11 inch sheet of plain white paper.

37

Gloria MacKay

I learned early not to question the art of a child. An expert on child rearing wrote a best selling book about parenting and I was reading the chapter on children's art. The author, Dr Somebody, advised when responding to a child's artwork pick one or two features in the picture that you sincerely like, make a positive comment and be done with it. In other words, don't insult the child with hyperbole.

As if on cue my five year old came to me holding out a drawing. "I've made a picture of you, Mommy." I put my arm around him, silently assessing the drawing and smiled. "I see you've drawn me wearing a pink polka dot blouse. I like that."

He jerked away and yanked the paper out of my hands. "Naw, Mom," he snarled. "Don't you know anything? Two's your buttons and two's your boobs."

What is it that we lose as we get older and why is it gone and how can we get it back? When Friedrich Nietzsche, an artist not with paints but with words and ideas, talks about creativity he says, "One must still have chaos in oneself to be able to give birth to a dancing star."

Literally we can do just that. Astrophysicists tell us that every nucleus of carbon in our bodies originated in the stars. We're stuffed full of stars. Now, if we can only get the children to show us how to make them dance.

A Conversation

If I could think just a little bit harder
feel just a whit more intense
care just a touch more
or, perhaps, a titch less
I think I would have it.

If I would pursue a romance
or learn how to tat,
manage to dance,
not be so fat
look good in a hat
Then I could get it, I bet.

It?

You know,
what everyone gets
when they get it.

I got it.

What is it?

It's optional.

Gloria MacKay

Just Around the Corner

I never heard music until I found jazz
Really heard it
Felt it
Loved it as though it were mine

Before jazz … the music, not the word, everyone
Knows jazzy, jazzed and all that jazz …
What with working all night and schooling all day
I was a zombie, a fool, I had no music

Hey, I couldn't carry a tune
I didn't play anything but the radio
Still can't. still don't
Can't even clap right, so said my friend

Maybe I didn't find jazz, after all
More than likely, it was jazz that found me
When you're marching and you're happy
Clap your hands
That's jazz
When you're dragging and you're bluesy
All alone
That's jazz

When you're great and when you know it
When you're beat and really show it
When you're quiet and tippy toe it
That's jazz

Who could have known
Jazz would literally be blown out of town?
No street to strut down, no place to play
We couldn't find jazz to save our souls

But jazz found us in a heartbeat
As long as we laugh, there is jazz
As long as we cry, there is jazz
Love, oh love, oh careless love

I Love a Parade

I like to stand right up in front
not so near my toes get trampled
by a marching band or my ears are
nearly in tears from the motorcycles

not that close. Nor caught unaware
by a shifting crowd, passing like
shadows on pavement. Not
that close. I stand with the watchers

alone and content, trading smiles
with mayors and queens, clapping for
the Flag, getting almost caught up
but not quite by the clowns.

When strangers throw candy I duck
My eyes define the shifting scene
like a picture frame keeping people in place.
I never edge inside. I do not touch. I watch.

Gloria MacKay

Table Talk

I was a quiet child.
Not being seen and not being heard
was not a rule I was raised by
but a condition I needed to thrive.

On special occasions I sat alone
under grandma's round oak table, tucked among
black oxfords and squeaky silk stockings,
as poker chips drop above me in muffled thuds
like big, wet snowflakes.

Not totally alone.
More like a house cat in a basket
or a footnote, squeezed under the important stuff
not yearning to be read — just happy to be there.

Every now and then an upside-down talking face
appeared. How ya doin', kiddo?
Don't look at me.
Are you asleep?
Don't look at me.

I muttered the same thing every time,
so I was told, no matter the question
no matter whose face.
They were probably right
Once, I remember
a hand crept in with a cookie
I took it.

A Cautionary Tale

Real time tosses us moments
like a handful of bees ... or corn
perhaps, popping,
lid slightly askew

Between the aim and the fire
the I and the do
the pitch and the hit and the woo
planes crash, hearts start,
bombs drop, legs cross

An unexpected moment
is as hard to grasp as a single tear
without a cheek,
a bead without a string
a q without a u

Dreamers beware, sleep as fitfully
as a new mother but rise like a sprinter
spring-set for gold, oblivious
to the ticks and tocks under their feet
real time flies

Gloria MacKay

Sunday Drivers Education

I presented to him the children, as pristine
as four chubby male bodies can be
elbows, ears, fingernails, toes
who sternly marches them to the car
slam bang honk honk

Bigheaded with rollers, half out of my robe
I tap the window, my tumbling hair
filtering his Sunday smirk. I'm coming,
I'm coming! I mouth with a shout
Honkety honk!

Alone, no longer behind before I begin
I am overly ready, quiveringly ready
sweaty earring denting my hand
and a honk stuck to my gut frozen
like yesterday's chopped liver

Opening Doors

I am glad I don't get sad when grayness muffles the days and it gets dark long before dinner. I scarcely notice, but some folks do. When daylight trails after the southbound birds and even dandelion down leaves town, they get depressed

Frankly, this surreptitious sliding of the seasons is not my favorite sleight of nature's hand. I love a syncopated beat: bouncing winds; dancing stands of evergreens; flashing fields of tulips by Seurat. But chains of days flattened by rain don't muffle my mood.

I glean enough brightness to move me along: shoes flashing as children trudge past, umbrellas of light on every front porch, three-way bulbs cranked on high. This is enough illumination for me, one who drives through fog with her sunglasses on and reads by a night light.

When the dark at the top of the stairs cascades like a waterfall, splashing shadows into sun-bleached corners, spreading a faded finish over sun-drenched drapes, and muting my yarn piled high in the corner looking garish and too hot to touch, I settle in to survive the gloom of gray days and return blooming like a Christmas cactus. Not everyone comes out of a closet so unscathed.

Gloria MacKay

The Family Album

Here I am boys, see, that's me
Standing tall, hands dangling
Eyes tight, don't laugh
The sun is in my face

Didn't you smile in those days, Mom,?

My smile must be hiding inside
Where no one can see it
Those are roses behind me
Climbing the fence
It is August the fifteenth
I am five now

What were you thinking, Mom?
She can't know that
She can't remember
She's just a little kid

I remember
I have to stand still
And wait for the click
And not talk
I hear two bees
But I am not supposed to move
I want my lemonade and cake right now
I don't want a scrap book

What's a scrap book?
Where are the rest of the people?

Mostly dead by now, I expect

Then, Mom, then
where are the rest of the pictures?

46

Oh, the roll?
you mean the rest of the roll
oh, I don't know
I was only five you know
They must be in here somewhere

Did you get a doll, Mom?
she doesn't know
I was only five
Mom, where is the rest of the roll?

Gloria MacKay

April at Home

Imagine springtime without baseball?
The season would be as empty as a hat
without a rabbit. Imagine a sunny Sunday
afternoon without baseball — the day would be
as incomplete as a deck of cards
without the ace of spades.

Fielders stand and wait while pitchers throw
and batters hit and run like crazy. That's the sport.
An occasional crack of bat smacking ball, followed
by all heads turned skyward, that's the magic.

We could fill our need for magic by wishing on stars
but when wishes get rained out they can't always
be rescheduled. We could develop a sixth sense
but can you take a sixth sense stretch? We could try
reading minds, but we don't know the signals.

If you don't remind me baseball is a business
not a sport, I won't remind you that baseball gives
memories to children. If you don't harp that baseball
is overpriced and slow-moving, I won't whisper that your
whole darn deck of cards is marked.

If you will look for magic in my five ounce leather ball stuffed
with cork and rubber and wool I will gaze into your big round
crystal ball and search for what I wait for all year long …
the glow of baseball that lights up the spring

A Friend Indeed

Some women I know
won't park in handicapped stalls
without a sticker — neither do I
but nowhere near the handicapped stalls?
Why?
I'm locking my car as one drives by
window open, pursed lips chirping.
Personally, I don't park this close to "them"
they might get confused
I see a spot up the hill at the end
no, don't bother to save me a seat.
I can stand.

Some women I know
don't say hello when they phone me.
You're busy. I can tell,
in the middle of dinner I bet.
Not yet.
You have company. I forgot.
No, I'm home alone.
Alone? It's Sunday.
I thought your children would be there.

Some women I know, not all
are martyrs with claws
and I am road kill;
they love me to death.
Everyone has to die of something
I am glad I'm not a cat.

Gloria MacKay

Out to Lunch

A still wind
slips in like a sigh
as stilted people
in straight-backed chairs,
flat napkins folded
on pre-hung laps,
speak silently.
A soft touching
curve tossing
shoe sparkling
claim jumping
eye-catching quiver
slides off a wink,
nudges a nostril,
tickles a dimple,
drops in my pocket
like an answer.
Our game is not
nil to nil anymore.

The Melt Down

After a defrosting night
Snow crashes
Old snow
Tired snow
No place to go but down snow
Morning sashays across our crazy quilt lawn
Ice dripping from her lashes
Snow in her toes

Across the street in the vacant lot
We call it the green belt
A cluster of unbending firs quivers while
Solid branches of ice break over our heads
Hitting the ground in hostile thuds
Like toddlers sprawled in the aisle
Relinquishing fistfuls of candy.
The party's over.

Gloria MacKay

Groping

where is the mind bleach
to lighten our dreams
and tie-dye soft shadows
among the dark scarves
of night?

a rasp, perhaps,
to dull the edges
of human tongues
still barbed after a half-life
of butt-ins and put-downs

best grab a wrap
stifle the subtle grind of abuse
from the hard drive of our souls
spinning slow, slower, slowest
with no place to go

Leg Stretching

I watched him strut
through his house of mirrors
like a witching stick
searching for confrontation

and so it goes: my shadow drifts
without motion down hallways
of gray with cautionary flickers
of lashes to lighten my way

Gloria MacKay

Out of Sight

Generally, 'lost' is a manner of speaking
not irrevocable
such as youth and yesterday
more in and out like the dog

retrievable: our tempers, our car keys, our place
even memories tug and run with the leash
of least resistance, misplaced with ease
but not forgotten

'Gone missing' is different
with its sibilant hissing of force or volition
run away, dragged away, hide away, put away
child's play, far away

gone … in a news flash, up a black hole
grab a hand, break a leg, bubbles popping
door locking … missing
overnight

night stalking
just walking
stars bright

I Am Paper

I am paper
He is scissors
Scissors cuts paper
I always have to be paper

I am paper
She is rock
Aha! Paper covers rock
I win

Scoldings from snickering spirits
smother my soul with post-it notes
Oops, rock covers paper
I am paper

Who will play their game when I die?
Who, then, will they cover and cut?
Hey, they might go first
I could write my own verse

If Popeye can boast
I y'am what I y'am
Why, then, oh why can not I?

Justa

They shocked me out of my socks as I passed by. The woman, all wrinkly and pinkly and permed, bracelets jiggling, fingers aglow, tips up her head and titters, "Are you absolutely sure she's justa friend?"

"Come along, sweetheart" he nudges. "Time for lunch. You know how cranky I get when I'm hungry."

As they sashay past her giggle grates my space. "So, she's a friend, nothin' to you, justa friend?"

When is a friend just a justa? The two shouldn't share the same breath. If you're a parent, of course, just a paired with minute is a dispensation allowing a few extra moments of peace. Just a minute. Justa minute, please. Now, justa darn minute.

Or when the birthday cake is served and I see one of those awful sheets slathered with frosting and embedded with golfers, ballerinas, or mice in street clothes I can speak with relief. "Justa little piece, please."

Or when coffee is served and we shouldn't have any more but it smells so good, we can beckon, "Justa half a cup, please."

She is justa friend, however, is like claiming the expression emanating from the Mona Lisa is justa smile or that I love thee, let me count the ways is justa start of a story problem.

Justa walk in the park? I don't necessarily reject a figure of speech. Justa little night music? I'll bend to that. Justa gigolo? Perhaps, but never justa friend.

Scadalogical

I've had scads of cats —
for instance, Bitchy Mama our ballistic
Balinese, and White Cat,
a playmate for the caterpillar

we named Bullet Bob Hayes
and O.J. of course, who came,
who strayed, who lost his way
not the shrewdest cat in the litter box

I must say, but only four sons
(a tad short of a scad
on the Richter scale for mums)
three who loved Pepper best

(sheesh not in a shaker, on a leash)
and he who slept with White Cat
or did not sleep at all
never take in a cat

I was warned belatedly
they leave scratches on the chairs
and hair everywhere.
Rather vexing

but more perplexing
are my sons who scratch like cats
but seldom shed
instead they claim they're texting.

Gloria MacKay

Pets Are Never Forever

For a while we had two pets
not when I was five
then there was just my dog Frisky
who ended dead under the laurel hedge
I was alone when I found him

Two pets when I was the mother —
the cat O.J. a baby we found on the porch
(he never did answer to Juice)
and Bob Hayes, a fuzzy black and orange
caterpillar we usurped from a sun-baked

football field on a Saturday afternoon.
Settled in his mustard jar, well-cushioned
with four little fists of grass, O.J. would roll
Bob Hayes across the carpet and down the hall.
Bob never answered to anything

Then came the days when our O.J. could
only make right-handed turns, making it
confusing for him to get out of the closet
where he slept. When I found him
behind the boots I was alone

The caterpillar, without instruction,
apparently learned how fly
one day the lid was askew
the grass in place but he was gone
the day I never found Bob Hayes
I was alone

Take a Chance

It's all in the timing
nods the mechanic to the blonde
who knows which paths are bricked in gold
but she's saving them for the starving children
chewing their shoes
on late night TV.

Up her sleeve, a bag of tricks
from the giggle store
cheaper by the dozen, less is more
what you see is
all in the timing.

Like the wobbly smile of a marionette
with no strings attached
stumbling over crumb prints
fresh or dry, sourdough or rye
she could just die.

Ma'am, not to be sarcastic
but what'll it be — paper or plastic
need a pen?
whatcha mean, when?

Gloria MacKay

It's Not Easy Being Nice

Nice is a word we use when we really don't care. A word we stick in a sentence when we need to fill space, like popcorn in a packing box or grated zucchini in chocolate cake.

A child makes a picture and rushes up with outstretched arms. This is for you! What do we say? Isn't that nice. What do we say to the butcher? A nice little rump roast, please. To the checker? Have a nice day.

When someone refers to me as nice, I scream inside with indecision: how do you know whether I am generally nice or nice only to you? Sometimes I am and sometimes I'm not. Does this make me a nice person part of the time or a partly nice person all of the time?

It's not easy being nice. What should a nice girl do when a guy tells her a not so nice joke (and it's really funny)? Should she laugh, snicker sheepishly or just stand there rolling her eyes in her niceness?

Nice is a do nothing word. Why must our tea be nice and hot; our milk, nice and cold; our beds, nice and cozy — when hot, cold and cozy would nicely suffice?

Even Sinatra, still flaunting his coolness, continues to croon let's take it nice and easy, when easy does it every time.

There Was a Baby Once

I feel disconnected living so high off the ground
as though I have misplaced something
like the baby.
I find myself hurrying in from the mailbox
listening for the baby
Throwing my arm across the car seat when I stop
groping for the baby
Sorting laundry hit-or-miss, not my usual style
Where is the baby's pile?
Where's his blankie, where's his smile?

There was a baby once
several, to be exact
in the play pen on the grass
Not in a bunch like rosy radishes
but one by one, as babies come,
and one by one, they go, I know
with lilac trees and shoes with cleats
packed with memories and last year's seeds

My mailbox has a number I can't begin to see
from three stories in the air
where I hang fuchsias on the deck
and watch the sun drop through the trees
and sniff as fragrances drift past
like babies footprints in the grass.

Gloria MacKay

Writer's Remorse

I can never say quite as much as I know
never recall all of a thought
never stick in my thumb
and pull out the whole plum

or describe quite as much as I know
Bits and pieces cling to my brain
like crumbs on a cupcake wrap
fall to wherever it is lost thoughts drop

ooze to another's mind
stick to another's page
I read it and groan
Why didn't I think of that?

Gray Saturdays

a tie …
snarls the coach
his team slumped in straggling rows
like string beans with their helmets off
… is like kissing your sister.

the parents …
crouched in the bleachers
sodden and grim,
bobble their heads,
as though dissing both kissing and sisters
… and sheepishly echo the beat.

Gloria MacKay

Mark My Words

If our world is to end up balanced
nothing awry
not in our world
not at the end, anyway, then
when you start talking religion … again
don't ask me if I believe in God, because
instead of getting an answer
I'll give you a question.

How are you defining God these days, eh?
This will ultimately upset the fine balance between
the ask and the you shall receive marks of punctuation.

Let us pretend I simply agree
there is such a one in whom I believe
You will assume my God is your God
(there is only one, eh)
He is in both of our heavens
so all's right with the world.
Amen.

Or She?

I am apt to answer a question with a question
even though I know that the final answer, like the cheese,
should stand alone at the end

but it won't be my fault
will it?

The Count Down

All twenty four of us ended up on the left of the center aisle, four to a bench, in prearranged positions — not alphabetically, but according to some designated plan of the court.

Shortly after eight in the morning we had wandered in one by one and spread out on either side of the courtroom. The aisle seats filled up first. First in, first out I surmised as I grabbed a prize spot and got settled, not sure what would come next.

Next the suits and the robe filed in. For the first business of the morning, the judge stood and slowly called out our names while we gathered our belongings and slid into the assigned seats as quietly as books on a shelf.

I slipped into the third row from the front, the second spot from the wall next to a pert woman in a becoming maroon woolen coat with lipstick to match and a flowing scarf, soon loosened and untied. On my right was a quiet but comfortable looking young fellow: brush haircut, jeans, casual brown cotton sweater. A gaunt man barely balancing on the edge of middle age settled in the aisle seat in front of me. In his white shirt, stripped tie and tan checkered jacket he was thin beyond belief.

Some of our group apparently knew each other; they swiveled around, smiling, waving, shaking their heads slightly as though to say what are you doing here or how is it that we have ended up here, out of context, together? I envied them their comfort in finding a familiar face.

Next came introductions: the judge in his robes and the two attorneys (the older, on the side of the defense, in a navy blue suit; the prosecutor, younger and taller wearing muted grayish brown). They started right in asking us questions although not as many as I expected and not very telling, at least to my inexperienced ear. They acted as though they already knew us from the information we mailed in weeks before.

Each of us was encouraged to speak at least once; a few talked quite a lot while others, like me, had to be encouraged with a direct question. The attorney in gray wondered if I thought the breathalyzer test was unfair considering not everyone reacts to alcohol the same way. I rambled something about it was probably the best we could do, just like we all have the same speed limits although some of us drive better than others.

It is no wonder my mindset was more on driving than drinking. I had just traveled rather briskly over fifty odd miles in the darkness of early morning on unfamiliar roads with more curves than a bag of pretzels to get to the courthouse on time.

Far sooner than I would have expected we were rustled out of the courtroom. "Remember your seats," chastened the judge. Just time to use the bathrooms, unkink our legs, smile at a stranger, inhale a few breaths of fresh air. In a very few minutes the call came to return to our seats.

The judge, without preamble, read out six names and thanked and excused the remainder. He spoke so quickly and quietly I wasn't sure quite what he said, except for one name. My name. No doubt about it, I had become one-sixth of a jury.

The frail man was not, the perky woman was not. I did not even notice their leaving. I focused on the five who remained. I was pleased the young man next to me was still there. Even though we did nothing but nod, he was the closest thing to a friend I had in the room. Directly in front of me was a quiet woman with a shiny gray pony tail trailing down to her waist clutching a yellow paperback book of puzzles under her arm. Earlier, as she took off her coat I couldn't help but notice her trim dark gray shirt was on backwards. Later on in the day she had turned it around.

The other jurors were behind me: an imposing, big voiced older man in a roomy white long sleeved pullover; a short, ruddy faced, stiff-mouthed man in a plaid shirt; a jolly woman who belonged to the voice I had been hearing. I don't know what they thought about me. We were strangers early in the morning in an unfamiliar place with an uncertain day ahead. That's all that I knew.

There was a lot of quietness in the jury room as we waited to be called. Sitting around the table just the right size for six, we were comfortable enough but silent. Plenty to think about. No reason to share. I can't believe I'm here, was what I was thinking.

When we were summoned into the courtroom everyone was standing to greet us and we all sat down together. Everyone being the judge, the two attorneys and the defendant, a smallish man in a dark red corduroy shirt. As I swiveled around on my cushy chair in the jury box I could see only the right side of his face as he sat stone like, staring straight ahead.

Our work as jurors was taxing but not arduous; early on we were given a break while discussions went on in the courtroom. Our little room already felt like home, a quiet place to reconnect fleeting impressions: the judge, immutable eyes behind dignified glasses; the prosecutor, the more restrained of the two; the defense attorney, more bustling; the defendant, as still as the air around him.

Back in to hear testimony from two sheriffs, a state trooper and a state toxicologist. Then out for a lunch break. It looked as though all six of us went our own separate ways. I found a Tai place near by with a table for one and a newspaper. Under the circumstances it was easy for me to follow our firm instructions — do not discuss the case with anyone, not with each other, not with anyone.

That's one commendable thing that must be said for our jury. We did not open up to each other: not one word, not a shrug or a frown or a smile. As we sat in our room (not locked in it was made clear, it was the rest of the world which was locked out) not once did we make anything but the smallest of talk. Not once did anyone foreshadow the future when we would have to agree or allude to the fact there was no majority rules option for us.

As the clock ticked through the afternoon and the rain clouds darkened it became clear we would be back the next day. Witnesses kept coming. Friends and coworkers testifying for the defendant. Pieces of evidence: a meal and drink tab; breathalyzer test results; police reports; photographs of a bar and the defendant's place of business. A display of the tools of his trade. A lecture on how acetones and hydrocarbons can affect a breathalyzer. At the end of the first day I finally saw the defendant full faced as he took the stand and faced up.

Decision making time did not come until the next day, late in the morning. I knew my bent but had no expectations for the rest of the jury. Normally I might have spent time on speculation but I was so preoccupied with the trial itself I hadn't given my fellow jurors much thought.

If asked to predict the outcome I would have imagined much dialogue, perhaps three of us on one side of the table and three on the other pulling strings, twisting, tying knots. All of us taking turns to talk, all of us listening to each other just as intently as we had listened in the courtroom. And when push came to shove, at the saying goes, I would have envisioned the blacks and whites of our six separate existences weaving together into a fabric we would unroll before the court. We would be quick. We all had homes to go back to.

I would have expected some of us to talk more, others to listen more. Some to give. Some to take. I would have thought the demographics would determine who would lean one way and who, the other. I would have imagined we would choose words which would fit nicely in each other's ears.

At worst I would have thought we would run quickly through the gamut of dribbles and double talk and nuances and fine points and what is reasonable and what is doubt and all the other posturing and histrionics which are part of talking things through. But, when time spoke our antennas would all pick up the same station.

Ten minutes together and I felt the walls vibrate around me. That's that. Slam dunk. Ten eyes turned to me for acquiescence. Five fingers pointed at me and four chairs retracted noisily from the table.

The man in the plaid shirt, the same man who had chatted with me about his vineyard, his native country, the same man who had confessed to me he had once reported a guilty party because he felt sorry for his children, this same man leaned forward and shot at my face some of the most vitriolic words which had ever come my way. Then he said he had enough of me, stood up and turned toward the wall.

At that moment the sandwiches came and that is how we ate lunch. I stared straight ahead, nibbled my tuna fish until I was not able to swallow, wrapped it up and stuck it in my purse. One way or another I knew I was going home soon and it was going to be a long, lonely ride.

By that time would I be the ostracized doubting Thomas who dug herself a hole and jumping in with both feet; the woman who wasted everyone's time and money because she didn't get it; the bimbo as dense as a black hole; the broad who couldn't tell Truth from a hole in the ground?

Or would I drive home basking in their glory. All I had to do is decide they are right. We would go in to the courtroom together, united and clear. Maybe he is guilty. It is a judgment call, like how high is an infield fly or how rare is the steak. They would be so proud of me and pleased with themselves.

The six of us might exchange email addresses and phone numbers. We would plan to have lunch together some day. Not that it would ever happen, but I wanted to be included in the fantasy. It would be something warm to think about on the lonely drive home.

The puzzle woman found a sharp pencil. The chatty woman talked non-stop as though she was the misbegotten hostess of an ill-conceived dinner party. The man in the plaid shirt stood and chewed. I could see his ears moving. "You are going to have to stand out there in front of everybody and say not guilty when the rest of us say guilty" he said. "They're going to ask us all, you know. They're going to know you are the one."

I looked at the young man, our foreman, and told him I had question for judge. He leaped up with a pencil and pad, trying his best to make us all come out even. When the world is locked out the way to ask a question is summon a messenger by phone, hold out the folded paper, close the door and wait for an answer. Twice I sent questions. Twice came answers.

Both times they strengthened the doubt in my mind. Which is strange, because both times these same responses confirmed the verdict of guilt in the five minds of my peers. They said I did not ask the right questions. Ask your own questions, I retorted.

There were five of them and only one of me. I knew I could never change all of their minds. Not if we never got home. Easier for them to change mine. Quick and easy. Who's to know?

I nodded to the young man and he knew it was time to do our work and move on. We were summoned into the courtroom and stood while the foreman read the verdict. Nobody polled the jury. nobody said anything. All we had to do was walk out single file leaving behind one judge, two attorneys and one defendant, still wearing his red corduroy shirt.

I did not lead the procession but somehow I was the first one out the door. The entrance was quiet, the parking lot motionless, but in the distance trees bent in the wind. I walked quickly without turning to wave goodbye.

I drove easily. It was stormy but still daylight and the stretch of windy roads felt familiar. By the time I got home my eyes were dry and my tuna sandwich was still on the seat beside me looking as limp as I felt. Limp without joy but limp without guilt. There is only the trip. One mile after another.

Keep in Touch

I never touched him
She hasn't touched her dinner
Don't be so touchy
My plane touched down without a bounce
others pierced the tower
like thread through the eye of a needle

touch off, touch up, touch base, touch wood
a lever on the back of my old black phone
slides from touch tone to pulse
What would happen if I switched off the touch?

Words slide from our tongues with more ease
these days, less disingenuous, less a facade
as though a smoke signal hovers above
in the manner of a wordless whisper

a laying on of a hand
a pat here and there but not everywhere
we have learned passion but also restraint
as though one must collect

a private reserve of who needs what
and who knows when
and where and why
Keep in touch

Gloria MacKay

Timelessness

Admittedly, my brain
is no place to camp out:
unsteady as a knuckle ball
frayed as old rope
as impervious to change
as the clock with no hands
my friend keeps on her mantel
because she likes chimes

A nervy curvy magic slate
has found a spot in here
my pain brailled
into the waxy black,
exuding stringy screams of glee
whenever the fragile sheet
is peeled away

Time, we find, stops ticking on its own
and can squeeze our space to nothingness
which is no more a surprise to me
than some closets I've called home.

Goodbye

Not usually a happy word
unless you're the one slamming the door.
At best an obligatory duet at the end of a chat
goodbye
goodbye
see ya
see ya
So much for that
movin' on

Some conversations plod through time
fraught with pauses
like pistons out of synch
oops call waiting
neighbor knocking
dogs barking
damn the buzzer, the beeper, the blink
gotta go
gotta pee
gotta gotta
'bye
'bye
Who says it first?
this means something

Even the best intended one-on-one
can blur like chiffon in the rain
leaving soft thoughts left unsaid
secrets withheld
tears disappeared
before they are able to drop
see ya
well ... bye
uh huh
oh my
soft sign
goodbye

Made in the USA
San Bernardino, CA
06 February 2017